Poems of Kamloops
& Beyond

Douglas E. Daws

TRAFFORD
PUBLISHING

USA • Canada • UK • Ireland

The tree which moves some
To tears of joy
Is in the eyes of others
Only a green thing
Which stands in the way.
As a man is, so he sees.

~ William Blake 1799

Note for Librarians: A cataloguing record for this book is available from Library and Archives
Canada at www.collectionscanada.ca/amicus/index-e.html
ISBN 1-4251-0485-1

Printed in Victoria, BC, Canada. Printed on paper with minimum 30% recycled fibre.
Trafford's print shop runs on "green energy" from solar, wind and other environmentally-friendly
power sources.

TRAFFORD
PUBLISHING™
Offices in Canada, USA, Ireland and UK

Book sales for North America and international:
Trafford Publishing, 6E–2333 Government St.,
Victoria, BC V8T 4P4 CANADA
phone 250 383 6864 (toll-free 1 888 232 4444)
fax 250 383 6804; email to orders@trafford.com
Book sales in Europe:
Trafford Publishing (UK) Limited, 9 Park End Street, 2nd Floor
Oxford, UK OX1 1HH UNITED KINGDOM
phone +44 (0)1865 722 113 (local rate 0845 230 9601)
facsimile +44 (0)1865 722 868; info.uk@trafford.com
Order online at:
trafford.com/06-2243

10 9 8 7 6 5 4 3 2

Acknowledgements

It is a masculine trait to not seek help, in anything less than dire circumstances. Thus it was for me in developing and putting together the poems in this book. Thankfully, my wife, Margaret Palmer Daws, knowing my reluctance to ask for help, recognized my confusion, and without being asked, took it upon herself to give invaluable assistance, resulting in the publication of this book of poetry. Her essential help is therefore acknowledged, with my humble thanks.

This book of poems is dedicated
To each member of my family.
My wife, my children, grand-children
And great-grand-children;
Who have provided me with the love
That has inspired me to write
Of the great joys of living.

About The Author

Douglas Daws, was born in England, at Grantham, in Lincolnshire, on August 30, 1920, but for the earliest years of his life, he lived in South London, the home of most of the Daws family.

A move was subsequently made to the small village of Hilton, in Huntingdonshire, where he began his schooling; schooling that continued in Lincoln, and Cambridge.

At the age of 19 years, in 1940, he, with most of his schoolmates, enlisted in the Royal Air Force, serving in various parts of the world, until June of 1946, when he was discharged. Having been married during the war of 1939-45, he and his wife immigrated, relocating in Canada, at Kamloops, B.C.,

In Kamloops, he had a successful career with the Federal Government, and with the City of Kamloops, where he was employed as Parks Manager, until retirement in 1982.

As a writer of poetry throughout his life, his writing became more prolific after retirement, and continues to the present, with his third book of poetry now published.

Affirmation

For if in any single day
You see a little child at play
Or watch a lovely butterfly
Or perfect rainbow in the sky
Or hear a bird sing in a tree
You're as rich as anyone can be

Chapter 1

GIFTS OF NATURE

*The great beauty of the forest
Displayed in shades of green
Illuminated by the morning sun
Is nature's perfect scene*

Contents

A Wild Creatures Home

Cyril the squirrel, ran through the forest,
The home of his family and friend,
Crying out words of greatest alarm,
About a bulldozer that signaled the end,
Of homes in the shelter of evergreen trees,
That supplied winter's food without fail.
Homes of many past centuries of squirrels,
Whose destruction, they cannot curtail.
Cried the squirrels, "O Cyril, what shall we do,
With the arrival of back-hoes, bulldozers too,
When trees start to fall with a crash and a roar,
As they fall on our homes on the forest floor?"
Said Cyril the squirrel, trying hard to be brave,
"Our homes are doomed, but our lives we can save.
So let us all get together, just as fast as we can,
And quickly come up with our survival plan.
We must think of our future, or for us it's the end,
Let's seek a new forest, but who can we send?"
With limited choices, they all thought it best,
To find a new forest, somewhere to the west.
Then Harry the hawk, came forward to say,
He had seen a fine forest, not too far away,
And he thought it could be a suitable place,
With evergreen trees and no shortage of space
While Charlie the crow, from a perch in a tree,
Cawed, "Bulldozers will win, we must all swiftly flee,
Or it's the end of the world for creatures like us,
Always minding our own business, not making a fuss,

Thinking that humans, in their dreams of a plot,
For building fine homes on a city-view lot,
Would think of earth's creatures, no matter how small,
Wishing never to harm them, or let dangers befall.
Constructing in places, where there'd not be a need,
To cut down a forest, a most insensitive, sad deed".
But with no other choices, but to hurriedly go,
To seek a new home before winter's first snow,
Abandoning places where they had been born,
With the snake and the mouse, the doe and her fawn.
So gathered together, in their sadness and sorrow,
Saying prayers for a hoped for happier tomorrow,
And a wish that they find, a safe new forest home,
Where man and his back-hoes, would leave them alone
Respecting that they, were all God's creatures too,
With a right to their lives, so unqestionably true.

A Winter's Reverie

O to walk those familiar trails again,
Smell earth made fresh by night-time rain,
See fleeting glimpse of white-tail deer,
As spring's first buttercups appear;
And hear the meadowlark in song,
On Dufferin Hill, for which I long.

Birthday Hike

It was the thirtieth day of August,
The day that I turned eighty five,
A good day for hiking the forest trails,
And for giving thanks for being alive.
In knapsacks we carried a picnic lunch,
Which we ate at a bench with a view,
Excited in thinking of what we might see,
Before our hike in the park was through.
And we saw the most beautiful butterfly,
As it perched on a trail-side bloom,
A breathtaking show of bright colours,
That defied the cloudy day's gloom.
And in the long grass of the meadow,
Alert, but not appearing afraid,
A young deer stood, in all its glory,
Nature's perfection, our Maker had made.

Crocus And Snowdrop

How I pity the poor dainty crocus,
Who is valiantly trying to bring,
All the joyful beauty of springtime,
Long before the arrival of spring.
With the fragile bloom of the snowdrop,
That droops its head on the lawn,
A contrast against the grasses' green,
In cold winds looking sad and forlorn.
These February day prima donnas,
Appear somehow or other betrayed,
By a sudden surge of winter's weather,
That has most of Victoria dismayed.

Cyril The Squirrel

A most welcome squirrel is Cyril,
Appearing several times every day,
Swiftly running along the top of the fence,
Eating nuts that he finds on the way.
He is seen at an early morning hour,
And at all times he knows I'm sure,
No matter how many nuts he's eaten,
There will always be plenty more.
He is a delightful source of pleasure,
With the quick body movements I see,
Constantly twitching his bushy tail,
As he peers through the window at me,
With an innocent look, that seems to say,
(Cheeks puffed up with nuts to digest),
"Many thanks for your thoughtful kindness,
And all the nuts you leave for your guest'.

Finches And Juncos

The friendly finches and juncos,
Are such a delightful sight to see,
On a cold, brisk winter's morning,
Flitting swiftly from tree to tree.
In a quest for a nourishing breakfast,
Of the bird seeds they have spied,
In a hanging wooden feeder,
That I see from my chair inside.
And gazing at God's tiny creatures,
I feel pleased that they have found,
A source of life-giving sustenance,
In the seeds that fall to the ground.
And as I sit in my indoor comfort,
Surrounded by most of life's needs,
I'm always thankful to be reminded,
God's tiny birds, in winter need seeds.

Forest Conquest

Men are cutting down the forest trees,
That proudly grow on Dufferin Hill,
And cutting limbs from trees still standing,
A sight that makes one feel quite ill.
Men with hard hats and sharp axes,
Dressed like combatants in a war,
Terrorizing all the forest creatures,
With a chain saw's deafening roar.
And with flame, smoke and indifference,
They sadly set ablaze a funeral pyre,
Of trees that served mankind so well,
As a welcome climate modifier.

Golden Season

Together we sat at the viewpoint,
Watching the world far below,
In the valley of the Thompson,
Where great rivers to the ocean flow.
Nurturing life at the water's edge,
Ensuring poplar leaves will form,
When with the advent of autumn,
Trees in bright gold they adorn.
In a miracle of nature's vast beauty,
On the river banks where they grow,
Stretching for far into the distance,
In a most spectacular autumn show.

Hummingbirds

With a lovely lady there beside me,
We sipped a fine glass of wine,
As the sun was just descending,
And our mood was just sublime.
We had talked of nature's glory,
The great beauty that it brings,
When to our surprise and wonder,
We heard the buzz of tiny wings,
And saw two rufous hummingbirds,
In their colours of brown and red,
Heading for the scarlet blossoms,
In hanging baskets above my head.
They hovered there for just a spell,
Feeding on blossoms they could spy,
And made a perfect evening more so,
For my loving companion and I.

June

Among many wonderful months of the year,
The most idyllic must surely be June,
With it's variations of sunny and rainy days,
Enticing beautiful roses to bloom.
It's when swallows fly low in the evening,
In their swift and graceful flight,
And when days are at their longest,
Offering maximum hours of delight,
To see the glorious sight of butterfly wings,
And watch hummingbirds darting about,
Amidst the lush bounty of garden flowers,
For this is June at its best, without doubt.

Master Of Nature?

It really hasn't a ghost of a chance,
The evergreen forest's fine tree,
Against the tragic onslaught of man,
Who has as his greatest desire to be,
Nature's skilful and confident master,
Judge of what for the future is best,
As the land's new grand designer,
With whom great power is possessed.
And who has for his greatest mission,
The necessary weapons for war.
But instead of the warfare's rifle,
There is for him a lethal chainsaw,
For what is a pretty safe operation,
As there's sure to be no return fire,
On this very one-sided battlefield,
When a guarantee is, the tree will expire.

Mount Paul At Christmas

It is with awe that I view the mountain,
Bedecked in its fresh fallen snow,
On pines that grow at random,
To theThompson Valley far below.
I like to write of mighty rivers,
Frozen now from shore to shore,
And the glorious eastern sunrise,
That will be seen for evermore.
I like to see nervous juncos feeding,
On seeds dropped to the ground.
Feel silence, brought by winter snow,
That muffles man-made sound.
For all this is found in Kamloops,
When Christmas Day is close at hand,
And skies are filled with twinkling stars.
Bringing Christ's great joy to all the land.

November

Fall days are growing shorter now,
With fewer hours of brilliant sun,
And yellow leaves on poplar trees,
Are earthward falling, one-by-one.
Migrating geese are on the river,
Where they will rest before they go,
On their long journey southward,
Escaping winter's cold and snow.
Remembered flowers in the garden,
Have sadly had their summer fling,
And all the bees and butterflies,
Have departed 'til next year's spring.

October

The curly-cups and goldenrod still bloom,
As October's autumn days draw nigh,
And the yellow flowers of rabbit-brush,
Will attract each person passing by.
The leaves of Saskatoon are shed,
But aspen show their shimmering gold,
As squirrels prepare for the winter ahead,
For October's scenes are a joy to behold.

Our Patio Garden

On a wooden deck, beside the fence,
Our own summer garden grows,
In red pots of clay, and every day,
Bright coloured blooms it shows.
A visual feast of joy and wonder,
Of many gorgeous flowers in bloom,
With bright smiling face of pansies,
That will erase all hints of gloom.
Geraniums are the featured stars,
In shades of red and pink and white,
Accompanying bacopa's trailing beauty,
Will be always sure to bring delight.
As will gorgeous blooms of fuchsias,
Which the hummingbirds adore,
And the coleus and white daises,
Red impatiens, and much more.

Pansies And Daffodils

Bright yellow pansies, golden daffodils,
And pink blossoms on each cherry tree;
On the celebration of St. Valentines,
Are quite the loveliest sights to see.
When in the island city of Victoria,
Where we strolled beneath the sun,
To view delightful harbour scenes,
Until the daylight hours were done.
Then in the magic of the evening,
With a crescent moon bright in the sky,
We walked the harbour walk again,
Clasping hands, my dear love and I,
And strolled the promenade with lovers,
Every one with joy-filled heart,
As they promised wondrous futures,
In which they would never, ever, part.

Rain On Dufferin Hill

The rain had washed the forest clean,
With Douglas fir now fresh and green,
And on a sun-warmed afternoon,
There's found heady scent of Saskatoon.
While from the earth, will swiftly grow,
Kind nature's Dufferin wild-flower show;
In colours yellow, pink and blue,
Confirming life is born anew!
As joyful birds, upon the wing,
Sing songs to herald in the spring.
So grand is nature's great domain,
Refreshed by welcome morning rain!

The Chestnut Tree

In October, the horse chestnut tree,
Becomes a vision of glowing gold,
As it prepares itself for winter,
In the sunny days of autumn's cold.
And with this grand act of nature,
Ripened conkers will be found,
To the great delight of squirrels,
With winter's food upon the ground.
And from the early days of springtime,
When glistening buds begin to swell,
Bursting forth with pink candle flowers,
And large palm-shaped leaves as well.
The chestnut trees of park or boulevard,
Provide in summer welcome shade,
A thoughtful gift for all mankind,
The Lord above has for us made.

The Garden

I made for my true love a garden,
A garden of many floral delights,
For the flowers that she has planted,
Will be a beautiful, colourful sight.
The plot is not really a large one,
In fact, at five by seven quite small,
But with its front of the house location,
Will prove an eye-catching picture for all.
And with these very well tended flowers,
In bright colours of red, yellow and blue,
There'll be joy in the hearts of passers by,
Having such magnificent flowers to view.

The Robins Return

Such a delightful sight was mine,
At dawn, following showers of rain,
For there, in a flowering cherry tree,
The robins had returned once again.
Back from a winter in warmer climes,
Bringing joy on a morning quite cold,
With a promise that spring will be early,
And more beautiful birds to behold.
Perched among cherry tree blossoms,
On branches that soon turn to green,
Sprouting leaves from swelling buds,
For a magnificent springtime scene.

The Seat At The Crest

The seat that I sat on was grungy at best,
But nevertheless, was a good place to rest.
Being quite black and ugly, a round from a tree,
That had been in a fire, or appeared so to me.
It sat at the crest of a grass covered hill,
A fine vantage point, to experience the thrill,
Of vistas of rivers, and valleys stretched far,
Which put in perspective, how minute humans are.
It's also a place of rare silence and peace,
For spiritual comfort, as troubled thoughts cease,
As the mind becomes cleared, of all of life's woes,
So that nothing but serenity ultimately shows.
Where a path to the future, is sought in a prayer,
For an all-loving Father, will be forever there,
To sit down beside me, on an ugly black seat,
And tell me His love, is strong and complete;
And in all of life's journeys, in joy or in sorrow,
His love will support me, in every tomorrow.

Voices Of Nature

We quite often walk in the forest,
Enjoying its picturesque trails,
Engulfed in its peace and serenity,
Thankful for quiet that prevails.
Except for the voices of nature,
As in the delightful song of a bird,
And music of wind in evergreen trees,
A most welcome sound to be heard.
And when we walk in the forest,
There is care to not break the spell,
Of great joy in the forest voices,
Voices of nature, we know so well.

Winter In The Forest

The wild creatures of the forest,
Will be quiet and peaceful now,
Apart from very noisy magpies,
Who fly high from bough to bough.
And maybe an active squirrel,
Who dares to leave a winter home.
But silence is the welcome friend,
With whom I wish to walk alone.
For in the silent days of winter,
With snow deep on the ground,
Most creatures of the forest sleep,
From them you will hear no sound

Winter's First Snow

Peering through my bedroom window,
In winter's early morning light,
I saw a scene of awesome wonder,
For deep snow arrived last night.
The pine and sagebrush hillsides,
Were transformed at Nature's hand,
To become a vision of great beauty,
As a white blanket fell upon the land.
And there was everywhere rare silence,
The silence which only snow can bring,
A most wondrous peace descending,
Over each and every living thing.
Yes! I viewed with great elation,
All nature's wonders I could see.
Here from my bedroom window;
Beyond the fence, the old pine tree.
With snowflakes floating earthward,
Like tiny fairies from on high,
As they danced their winter ballet,
For this peaceful land to beautify.

Chapter 2

LOVE'S MUSINGS

It's not only when you're sweet sixteen
That cupid comes a'calling
In later years forget your fears
It could be in love you're falling

Contents

A Glorious Dream

I thought there'd never be a chance,
Something that just could never be,
That I'd find a sweet and loving lady,
Who would fall in love with me.
But I'm thankful it did so happen,
It gives me the utmost joy to say,
And we have now been married,
Exactly two wonderful years today.
Two years full of idyllic happiness,
In a life like a glorious dream,
Each day, a day of great harmony,
Every hour a grand moment serene.
I know I've been blessed by my Maker,
Who sent me a perfect angel to love,
Someone I'll always honour and care for,
As sure as stars fill the skies up above.

A House Of Love

Ours is a house that's filled with love,
Where harsh words don't belong,
A house that's filled with memories,
Of frequent laughter, joy and song.
This is a house that's snug and warm,
When harsh winter brings its chill,
Where I can sit by a cosy fire,
With my true love beside me still.
This is a house with open doors,
Where friends and family meet,
And where they reminisce together,
About days past, so rich and sweet.
I dwell in a house with my only love,
A truly treasured and loving wife,
Enjoying wonderful days together,
As I shall, for each hour of my life.

Been There – Done That

I see the young lovers of today,
Light-hearted, as they walk my way,
Bright eyed, caring not that I may see,
Their fond caress, hear words of glee.
Hand-in-hand, they walk on air,
Assured, possessing youth's own flair.
And thus it was, in years long past,
My memories flooding back so fast!
Of our strolls down many avenue,
And leafy country lanes we two.
With never doubt of futures grand,
Spontaneous was our clasp of hand.
Oh yes! I often felt my passions rise,
As I looked into your pale blue eyes,
And did not care who overheard,
Words of love, your nearness stirred.
I have no wish for youth again,
Content to be a dimming flame,
For I still know that hand so dear,
That I may clasp, with sorrow near.
Now avenues and walks have gone,
This deepest love for you lives on.

Birthday Dilemma

There has come the day, for me to expound,
To speak soft words, with romantic sound,
For this is a day, which comes once a year,
The birthday of one, whose love is sincere.
So the words I say, must be honest and true,
Straight from the heart, a prerequisite too.
I considered a treat, a gift that's quite grand,
Or a fine restaurant dinner, specially planned.
But the eloquent words, I can't seem to find,
So to have dinner at home, I'm feeling inclined.
Which will solve a dilemma, do things up right,
As I tell you I love you, and cook dinner tonight.

Dream Wishes

I wish you calm and peaceful sleep,
Without the need of counting sheep,
A down-filled pillow, for your head,
And gentle waves to rock your bed.
With pastoral visions in your dreams,
And softly flowing, languid streams,
Where graceful swans float idly by,
Beneath a lover's moon on high.
Then in the morning mist, a fawn,
To share with you a glorious dawn.

Flowers Mean Love

I love to bring you flowers from my garden lady fair,
And place them oh so gently, in your soft and lovely hair;
Where the pansies will be happy, to rest upon your head,
With a rose's velvet petals, sharing perfume gladly shed.
I love to bring you flowers, as I have for many a year,
To see again in your sweet face, a glow of love so clear.
And I know until the day I die, a flower's form and grace,
Will be the symbol of my love, that nothing can replace.

Forgetting

Sometimes I know, I do fail to say,
"I love you dearest, so much each day"
And sometimes too, I will forget,
To say "you're ever lovelier yet".
Or simply, "I'm so truly sorry sweet",
When making comments indiscreet.
But then quite often, I'll bring a rose;
Or write romantic words in prose,
Which try and tell you sweetheart mine,
My love for you, is for all time.

I'll Not Miss You

I did say that I'd not miss you,
When agreeing we should part,
But I still have a desperate longing,
Within this aching, grieving heart.
To me, our parting was not easy,
Although I said "I don't really care,
If there's another love you've found",
But you failed to notice my despair.
Of course I said I wouldn't miss you;
For I knew no other words to say.
And then I tried to show indifference,
As you turned, and walked away.
That's about as truthful as me saying,
I cared not if song birds ceased to sing,
Or if the sun should never rise again,
And the heavens cold darkness bring.

I Wonder

How would it be I now wonder,
If by chance we had never met.
Would stars shine just so brightly?
Would the sun at evening set?
And would hibiscus never bloom,
The scent of roses fade away?
Would rainbows never grace the sky?
The sun not rise at break of day?
To you my dearest heart, I tell,
And to my only love, I cannot lie,
With you not by my side each day,
The moon would never light the sky.

My Patient Love

I know I go on at length, in a tedious way,
About the state of the world, as I see it today,
After hearing reports on the radio news;
(As an unwanted critic, with prejudiced views)
About feminine groups crusade against males,
And the incessant sports, that nothing curtails.
Yet the lady I've loved, for over two years,
Just never responds to my prejudiced smears,
Never remarks, just how tiresome I've been;
Showing great patience, instead of a scream.
And by her demeanour, at my oral display,
She must really love me, despite things I say.

Nocturnal Reveries

At the end of each day, as I seek out my bed,
A place where sweet memories enter my head,
In those nocturnal moments, that in-between time,
With memories of you, your hand clasped in mine.
Not conscious of place, and not yet asleep,
Those romantic memories do stealthily creep,
Flooding my mind, as an ocean's strong swell,
About moments of love, we both knew so well,
With thoughts of a lifetime, of infinite joy,
A love so great, passing time cannot destroy.
With you in each scene, of a fairy-tale dream,
Close in my arms, as you have so often been.

Pillowcase Roses

A silent symbol of my love, the rose,
Its beauty oft described in poetry or prose,
Is nature's vain attempt, to you outshine,
My dearest love, who made my life divine.
I still see pale roses on the pillowcase,
Where each night, would rest your lovely face:
You'd grasp my hand, as sleep drew near,
And murmur softly "I so love you, dear".
Then as morning came, for each new day,
With sleepy voice, I would hear you say,
"I forever wish, to wake with none but you"
And we would share a kiss, as fond lovers do.
The roses on the pillowcase will fade away,
But the rose left in my heart, will forever stay.

Saint Valentine's Sunset

The sub-tropic sun of early evening,
Sinks quickly to beneath the sea,
To give its daily blazing exit bow,
For viewers on the beach with me.
You will know those who are lovers,
For they clasp each other by the hand,
Then slowly walk in mystic moonlight,
Along Waikiki Beach's golden sand.
Each one confessing to a life-long love,
On this most special lover's day,
The day that is for Saint Valentine,
When to your love, sweet words you say.

Sure Love

This great love for you, is just as sure,
As the coming of each years spring,
When fragrant lilac blossoms bloom,
And gay feathered birds will sing.
And my love for you, is just as sweet,
As the sweet nectar from a flower,
And for every day that passes by,
Grows so much sweeter every hour.
My love for you, is strong and true,
A love that will surely weaken never,
Growing stronger every passing year,
Binding firm, the two of us together.

Tell Me You Do

Please tell me you love me, tell me often you do,
And I will truthfully answer, I truly love you.
Tell me you're happy, each time we embrace,
So I'll always remember, the smile on your face.
Tell me it's thrilling, when sharing a kiss,
Like being in heaven, on a love seat of bliss.
Repeat many times, as I hold your soft hand,
That the fire of emotion, is so speedily fanned.
So I'll never forget, in the days we don't meet,
Your beauty and grace, as my heart skips a beat.
And when I'm alone, feeling quite sad and blue,
I'll have sweet memories, to remind me of you.

Velvet Night

O velvet night draw on, your darkness hides my tears,
And brings me dreams, which sooth my lonely fears.
O welcome night draw on, my wish for every day,
But hours of daylight slowly creep, as I plead for no delay.
There is a well remembered place, to visit in the night,
Its there I always find you, in scenes of past delight.
When I first found great love, the vision that is you,
In your broad brimmed hat, and dress of angel's blue.
O velvet night draw on, I need your arms around me now,
With the comfort of your hands, upon my troubled brow.
Your lips to meet with mine again, as sweetly as before,
As I told you of a forever love, for the one that I adore.
O healing night draw on, for the light of day brings pain,
As it always will, until I'm home, safe in your arms again.

We Did Too

Some love stories begin, on the very first line,
With the simple words, "Once upon a time".
And I see no reason, why I should deviate,
For this true love story, I shall now relate.
My tale transcends time, back to forty one,
When a glorious romance, had just begun,
Between a beautiful girl, Madge was her name,
And a young RAF man, at whom Cupid took aim.
Each day of a courtship, was a breath-taking dream,
Every wonderful hour, a grand moment supreme,
As they cycled the trails, and byways together,
In the summer's delightful, bright sunny weather.
It happened by chance, a spill to the ground!
Then a tender scene, as the hurts were all found.
An opportune time, for a swift moment of bliss,
With the balm for the pain, a hug and a kiss.
And nature was kind, was a thoughtful giver,
Arranging for ice, on the Saskatchewan River,
For them to go skating, each fine afternoon,
With never a wish, to leave skating too soon.
And then, hand-in-hand, they took the walk home,
To a place of warm comfort, the two all alone.
It was there they would dream, as most lovers do,
And plan for their future, the life they'd pursue.
Then, as in all good love stories, if the loving is true,
They married, living happily ever after, and we did too.

When You're In Love

When you're in love, there should be joy in your heart,
But for me, that cannot be, as we are so far apart;
My heart is now heavy, I'm feeling wretched and blue,
With thoughts of long months waiting, until I'm with you.
Your letters are helpful, and bring you closer to me,
But it's really your beautiful face, I long to see;
Last seen, as the train, from Deal station was starting,
When I stifled my tears that came at our parting;
And I certainly know, I shall weep once again,
As I see my dear love, from the returning Deal train.

Chapter 3

MEMORIES

Memories are something to treasure
Of places and events of the past
And some will have made an impression
That to the end of your days will last

Contents

Ainahau - Home Of A Princess

Most treasured place on all the earth,
This isle of Princess Kaiulani's birth.
And there she had a home, a shady bower,
Another Eden, known as Ainahau.
And nestled where the date palm grew,
This house of love, the princess knew,
Safe there, beneath its wooden beams,
The royal child could dream her dreams.
She could hear at dusk a peacock's cry,
As if to grieve that night was nigh;
Saw mystic moon rise, from her bed,
As shadows danced on Diamond Head.
Oh Ainahau, she knew you so well,
Spent happy years beneath your spell,
Your banyan's cool and welcome shade,
Sweet comfort, for the little maid.
Where at your ever-open gate,
No guest would ever need to wait,
And children's laughter, filled the air,
Beneath great banyan's shelter there.
While she, as happy children play,
Picked blossoms for the luau's lei;
Hibiscus for her dainty brow,
At Ainahau – at Ainahau.
There on those pathways, lush and green,
This child, who would be one day queen,
Her pony rode with joy and grace,
With wind-swept hair about her face.

But days of childhood, of dearest friend,
Were days the princess knew would end.
Then came at last that fateful day,
When she would sadly sail away,
To leave behind for many a year,
That loving home she held so dear,
No more to feel the trade winds blow,
Or see the golden sunset's glow.
And from the ship far from the shore,
With tearful eyes, her home she saw,
Then gave a solemn, sacred vow,
To come back home, to Ainahau!

Bewitching Gibsons

I sat out on the deck for dinner,
At the end of a most perfect day,
From where, across rippling waters,
I viewed the ferry from Horseshoe Bay.
The evening was sublimely peaceful,
Not a cloud could be seen in the sky,
A sign that tomorrow would bring again,
Great delight for visitors here, such as I.
When I'll see more of bewitching Gibsons,
Its harbour, picturesque sail boats as well,
When I stroll on the glorious sea front,
Captured by Gibsons magical spell.

Gibsons Morning

The misty waters of the morning,
Reflect the glow of rising sun,
To bathe the sea in radiant glory,
For another day had just begun;
A new day for geese a'feeding,
On the lush grass of the green;
And appearing in the garden plots
The robin, finch and jays are seen.
Sunrise hours are for feathered friends,
In which to greet the dawn with song,
As has been done for untold years,
When sunrise beams grow strong.
And making sure the world awakens,
The seagulls, as is their morning norm,
You'll hear shrieking loudly overhead,
As they announce another day is born.

Hawaiian Magic

The magic of this island chain,
Compels me to return again,
To live with sun, blue sky and sea,
With treasured friends in Waikiki.
For there can be no other land,
So richly blessed by nature's hand,
And there's no other place I've seen,
With swaying palms in every scene.
And when I try with searching mind,
For grander memories I can't find,
A place where bougainvillea vine,
Display fragile beauty so divine.
And where each day hibiscus new,
Replace a flower, whose glory's through.
Or where the grand plumeria bloom,
Brings on the wind its sweet perfume.
Thus, if I had one choice, no more,
I'd forever choose Hawaii's shore,
Where I'd drown my senses, every one,
In Hawaii's magic 'neath Pacific sun.

Molly's Reach Memories

Off to Molly's Reach at lunch time,
That's where we all planned to go,
To live again sweet memories,
Of those happy years so long ago.
When we were all much younger,
The time when life was simpler too,
For parents and their children,
Who found pleasant things to do.
With walks beside the harbour;
A wharf, they found appealing,
Where children fished for shiners,
Their excited voices joys revealing.
There were the sailings of the Smokwa,
As infrequent as they were,
Unloading cars and passengers,
Which would always cause a stir;
Passing JohnWood's hardware store,
And climbing up the Gibsons hill.
But now, though the ferry doesn't come,
Gibsons lovers will keep arriving still.

My Beech Wood

When I was just a growing boy, of nine or ten or so,
A friendly beech-wood, was my favourite place to go.
I got there very quickly, along a footpath plain to see,
Through a meadow, and a hedge hole, located by a tree.
I'd pass a flooded chalk pit, next to the trail on the way,
Where a raft upon the water, was a forbidden place to play.
Then travelling on, across a lane, and up a grassy rise,
I'd see my inviting beech wood, so welcome to my eyes.
The wood was not a large one, but an ideal place to come,
For in branches high above me, squirrels had their fun.
The friendly rabbits watched me, as I walked into the wood,
And a crow gave caws of greeting, as it usually would.
It was a normal habit, to sit with my back against a tree,
And really try my hardest, to be as still as I could be,
For if I made no movement, forest creatures would appear,
And my wait would be rewarded, by a squirrel coming near.
Scurrying swiftly from tree to tree, then to the forest floor,
Busy gathering beech nuts, to add to its secret store.
I would see the doves and finches, in a never ending quest,
Collecting food for hungry mouths, awaiting in their nest.
And on one occasion I will mention, a creature came in sight,
Appearing from a nearby hole, to give me quite a fright;
When looking at it closely, I could see its two front paws,

And knew it was a badger, by its very lengthy claws.
So I sat there without moving, until the moment when,
The badger did a slow return, to its subterranean den.
Many are tales I could tell, about my favourite wood,
Imagining adventurous fantasies, about brave Robin
Hood,
Or Bonnie Prince Charlie, who fought the good fight,
To gain the English throne, with all of his might.
My beech wood was more than a good place to play,
And my experiences there, are rich in memory today,
So now that you know, of my early life as a boy,
I hope your life has a beechwood, for you to enjoy.

Tea With Merilee And Joy

It was a delightful location, for afternoon tea,
On the Moana verandah, overlooking the sea;
A tranquil oasis in a banyan's cool shade,
And Hawaiian minstrels, with a sweet serenade.
We were efficiently served, by a lady of grace,
Which was fitting indeed, for a superlative place,
And the Darjeeling tea, was simply supreme,
As were the scones, strawberry jam and cream,
Plus sandwiches made, by an artistic hand,
And pastries all served, in a manner quite grand.
All resulting in pleasures, which stay in my mind,
Of two lovely ladies, who were thoughtful and kind.

The Surf Room

We didn't come to buy expensive clothes,
Or to go to those Hawaiian Luau shows,
Nor to take a sunset dinner cruise,
Or spend our cash on nightly booze,
And buy pink pearls and golden rings,
Or the International Market's other things.
But we do love to come to dinner here,
During winter stays we take each year,
With Raymond as our gracious host,
In the dining room we like the most,
Where gourmet meals bring such delight,
And always appease our keen appetite.

Waikiki

How delightful to sit on the morning lanai,
As the sun's early rays beam from the sky,
Awakening birds asleep in the tree,
Who sing sweet songs with such gaeity.
Then soon to appear on the street below,
The every-day start of a constant flow,
Of walkers and runners, joggers as well,
In a pursuit of fitness, in the shortest spell.
And as the sun rises, the hum of the night,
Increases in volume, as there comes into sight,
Trash trucks and limos, and buses galore,
Hauling half awake tourist, on an island tour.
There is reasonable peace in the afternoon,
For just a short time, but ending too soon.
Then as the sun sinks, into an ocean of blue,
The noises of morning, are repeated anew.
As the extra-wide sidewalks, to capacity fill,
With the evening's strollers, seeking a thrill,
From sundry entertainers, artist and clowns,
Loud vocal preachers, having righteous frowns,
At the antics of revelers, all having their fun,
As a night full of pleasures, at last has begun.
The evening hours pass, with hope of some peace,
When the noises of day, diminish, then cease,
Letting birds sleep again, in the ficus tree,
Now the day is complete, in bustling Waikiki.

Chapter 4

RANDOM THOUGHTS

If you observe the world around you
With a keen discerning eye
You'll see a land of treasures
That money cannot ever buy

Contents

A Gift From Above

They made just an everyday coffee hour,
An occasion of considerable pleasure,
Three mothers with three little children,
With each one a veritable treasure.
I was seated alone, but not for too long,
When to my joy, they came into view,
And glad that I was to see them there,
For a mother and daughter I knew.
Such magical moments, I'll never forget,
Where "Second Cup" dispenses good cheer,
And has an enormous attraction for me,
As quite often some friends will appear.
Those bright happy faces of little girls;
And I'm including the newest ones too,
Gave my spirits a lift when needed,
For my mood was most decidedly blue.
With reluctance came the hour to leave
Still filled with a strong feeling of love,
I had found with the mothers and children,
Most assuredly, a great gift from above.

A Sea Princess Dinner

We were the envy of all those around us,
For our bearing and good looks as well!
And all that is without really trying,
Which proves again breeding will tell.
But apart from our charm and graces,
And the elegant way that we dine,
The stewards will tell, if you ask them,
It's in our oration that we really shine.
Our conversations are witty and daring,
Not a topic are we scared to touch;
Full of eloquence, wisdom and learning:
Little wonder we are envied so much.

An Eggsplosion

We planned for the day, in a bright happy mood,
Including desire, for some nice luncheon food,
And as we had eggs, in an ample supply,
It was thought hard-boiled eggs, in a salad we'd try.
So six white extra large eggs, went into a pot,
On top of the stove, with a setting medium hot.
Our morning's first stop, was the usual place,
For our Second Cup coffee, at a leisurely pace.
Then on to St. Paul's, for church business there,
Then on to the courthouse, a name change to declare.
But crossing the street, a thought entered my head,
About eggs on the stove, which filled me with dread!
A quick return home, was thought then most wise,
And what we found there, was in no way a surprise,
Finding exploding eggs, had spread debris quite well,
Plus filling the house, with an unpleasant smell.
The tiny egg fragments, did not look good at all,
Where they were spread, on the floor and the wall,
To this scene we had choices, for tears or for laughter,
But it was humour we saw, as we have ever after,
As in the kitchen we stood, in the midst of the mess,
Hugging and laughing, thinking it funny I guess!

Beautiful Music

My life has been all beautiful music,
Played in a great symphony hall,
By a magnificent world class orchestra,
The Maestro? The Lord of us all.
With rhapsodies, and concertos,
Tone poems and nocturns galore,
And all of this beautiful music,
From a perfectly wonderful score.
The Maestro still picks up His baton,
Every day as I wake up at dawn,
To continue a life-long musical work,
As He has, since the day I was born.

Christmas Spirit

I've seen so many happy children, in the busy shoppers throng,
And a lovely Christmas Pageant; heard a choir's voice in song.
I've seen a bright-lit Christmas tree, with a star upon the top,
With sparkling bells and baubles, that came from Santa's shop.
I've seen many acts of kindness, as Christmas Eve draws near,
Heart-warming signs of loving, when smiling faces will appear.
The season is not just for shopping, there are many gifts to give,
And the greatest gift of all is love, and being able to forgive.
There is the caring for each other, the offer of a helping hand,
For those in need are many, in the richness of this land.
With a joyful Christmas feeling, I arose from bed this day,
To find a gift of cake and cookies, in a plastic covered tray;
Placed carefully on the table, that sits by my front door,
A present from a thoughtful lady, a gift she'd made before.
I'm glad my friends and neighbours, show for me they care;
And know with Christmas coming, I could easily despair.
I'm thankful for this kindness, for a Christmas spirit shared,
Which made my Christmas happy, because of those who cared.

Dawn By The Window

The music of Delius, a bird's song at dawn,
Is surely perfection, as a new day is born.
A blue morning glory, asleep through the night,
Awakened by sun beams, is an instant delight.
Dew covered roses, the queen of all flowers,
Readies her blooms, for daylights bright hours.
And the fairy-like flight, of a butterfly,
Will now and then catch, my seeking eye.
All this beauty and wonder, has filled my soul,
And joyfully now, their glory is mine to extol.

Glory Days 1940

The hair recedes upon my head,
Where Brylcreem wave has long since fled,
There are some furrows on my brow,
While my vision's dim, and clouded now.
And well noticed is my creaking knee,
When rising from a low settee.
While much too often I forget,
The name of friends I've often met.
But look again! And you will see,
This youthful heart inside of me.
A heart that raced at "Bombers Moon",
As sirens wailed their mournful tune,
And Airforce boys would bravely go,
To try and intercept the Nazi foe,
In sturdy kite, with spirits high,
To challenge fate in night-time sky.
Now, for a cause that's just and true,
I'm sure my heart would race anew,
That I would heed my country's call,
With ageless spirit, straight and tall.
So heed not failing sight and ear,
Or notice memory less than clear,
But see this 1940 heart race on,
Although those glory days are gone.

Memorial Hill

With lowered flag and trumpet call,
A poignant peace falls over all,
Who stand in silence on the hill,
Proud veterans in the autumn's chill.
With reflective faces, lined by years,
Not shamed in shedding silent tears,
For friends that they will see no more,
With thoughts of cruel and heartless war.
Again the trumpet's call is heard,
And dormant spirits quickly stirred,
As the Maple Leaf lifts to the sky,
Where it should always rightly fly.
A sure sign of freedom to behold,
Not earned by power or nation's gold,
But by the blood of fine young men,
And thus "We shall remember them".

My Emotions

I can't imagine food without flavour,
Food lacking any discernable taste,
It would be without any pleasure at all,
A disappointing and terrible waste.
And thus it must surely be with me,
Admitting I am always in need,
Of food for the soul called emotion,
A desire I have no wish to impede.
For without the emotions from music;
From nature and faith as I write,
Then my soul without food of emotion,
Would suffer a sterile, unwanted blight.
I would never taste the salt of a tear,
Or quickening rate of adrenalin's flow,
When being rejected or falling in love,
Or hearing beautiful music I know.
So to try and curb my emotions,
Is an impossible and unthinkable plan,
For I would become a disciplined person,
An uninteresting and unhappy man.
Thus to change is out of the question,
I shall remain what I've always been,
A poet, a lover, a most sensitive soul,
Who chases the impossible dream.

Our Dinner Party

We're such wonderful, wonderful people,
But each with a large cross to bear,
Trying hard to bring culture and learning,
To the masses who really don't care.
We well know that our task is a big one,
And that progress is bound to be slow,
It could be that it's not in our lifetime,
That the slightest improvement will show.
But we shall continue to show by example,
The proper way nice people dine,
By using a wide range of expressions,
When we're testing new bottles of wine.
We shall always control our emotions,
And just never let snobbery show,
For we know our reward is in heaven,
As that's where really nice people go.

Santa's Happy Place

It is surely the happiest place to be,
For many small children, on Santa's knee,
In the centre court, of the Aberdeen Mall,
With bright coloured balls, both large and small,
Hanging from trees, and on a reindeer's rack,
Who is driving an engine, without any track.
And a reindeer is astride, a gay rocking horse,
Two more have trumpets, not playing of course.
With all of the magic, that Santa Claus brings,
Grownups not knowing, of such secret things!
Full of wonder and joy, are the children there,
Upon Santa's knee, in his official red chair,
With hope they'll remember, their lengthy list,
Dreading to think, a gift would be missed.
To Santa's question "Have you really been good?"
Is the predictable answer "Just as good as I could".
Their visit to Santa, for these girls and boys,
Have innocent minds, knowing elves make the toys,
While it's Santa who, in some mystical way,
Delivers on time, with his reindeer and sleigh.
So anxiously waiting, they now want to know,
"How many more sleeps, and will there be snow?"

The Cost Of War

A simple child, clad in her only dress,
No more knows a mother's love, or dad's caress.
An innocence, that only in our children shows,
Is no more; she lies in blood-splattered clothes.
From high above it came, from a Boeing 52,
A button pressed, by its high-tech crew.
Then from the sky, the killing means descended,
With no thought of lives, that would be ended.
"Our cause is just!" they voice the claim,
"With collateral deaths, there is no blame".
These airborne knights, led by those in power,
Hold in their hands, for each day's hour,
The lives of children, who may surely die,
From those death machines, securely high.
And in an oval office chair, does someone care?
There can be no victor, no victory in obscene war,
When the frightful cost, is children we adore;
Who have a right to life, to laugh and play,
A right for children, of their own some day.

The Farmer's Market

You'll find a block sealed off on Seymour,
Where at eight on a Saturday morning,
People bring sumptuous wares to town,
From homes they had left before dawning.
They have on view, on tables and trucks;
And open car trunks have revealed,
A wide arrangement of products to sell,
Fresh from their gardens and field.
There's a steady demand for young lettuce,
And strawberry rhubarb in season,
As there is for tempting spring onions
With freshness and flavour the reason.
Ladies are eager to buy the bedding plants,
While perennials attract them for sure,
With their plan for a beautiful garden,
To be one-up on the gardener next door.
There are always such delicious aromas,
From the bread and buns one will see,
That weakens resolve for a slimming diet,
But will bring to taste buds a great ecstasy.

The Golden Cherubim

When first I saw this little one,
This charming fair-haired child,
She couldn't know the joy she gave,
To a stranger when she smiled.
And as the days moved onward,
I hoped to see this child once again,
And cheered was I, and lucky too,
For those hopes proved not in vain.
For I saw her once again last Friday,
But I did feel quite saddened to see,
The fair-haired child was ailing,
And she was unable to smile for me.
I pray that soon she will be better,
And regain her infectious grin,
So that I may feel great joy again,
Seeing a smiling, golden cherubim.

The Perfect Time

The perfect time when I was young, was on a sunny afternoon,
Punting on the River Cam, to the outer world immune,
With an undergrad from Newnham, who I wanted to impress,
By performing feats of poling, with smooth and absolute finesse.
The rented punt from Granta Place, was at a horrid cost,
But needed to impress the lady, or the afternoon was lost.
I polled along serenely, for I was young and brave and free,
Confident in the good life, for to the door I had the key.
Then tied up beneath some willows, for a picnic hamper treat,
Of cakes she had provided, with some bread and potted meat.
We did things young people do, a hug and careful kiss,
On cushion enhanced comfort, for those moments of sheer bliss.
We listened to Debussy, on a wind-up gramophone at hand,
Or dance music from Sylvester, or a popular U. S. band.
But too soon a sad farewell was said, back at Granta Place,
With no future date suggested, though there was a nice embrace.
She then rode off upon her cycle, and I sadly rode off on mine,
After that punting day with Barbara, that surely was sublime.

The Tragedy Of War

The years have passed since ninety one,
And yet another bloody war's begun,
With all it's tragedy of death and pain,
From the callous hands of man again!
The innocent, as has been seen before,
Helpless victims in this mindless war,
In a nation's lust for power and greed,
Not restricted by just or honest creed.
Just oft said words "The cause is right,
Our power will surely win this fight".
So humble homes, in ruins where they fell,
Victim of smart bomb or high explosive shell.
Productive land, scorched by fiercest flame,
From where life-sustaining food once came,
Now sterile, it can no longer feed the poor,
By actions of an unseen airborne warrior.
Victims too, are parents of a well-loved son,
Whose dead body cannot care, which side won.
On Thanksgiving Day, for what do we give thanks?
For guns and ships? For planes and tanks?
How many see a young grandson at his play,
With dread, his call to war will come one day!

Wednesday Mornings

I find myself disliking Wednesday mornings,
For it's the time for a visit from hell.
When ground-keepers arrive with equipment,
Which make noises that nothing will quell.
The hearing attack starts at eight AM,
With a man and a hand-held machine,
Trimming short the long grasses edges,
With an infernal gas motors scream.
Then comes the high powered mowers,
That makes the ground shake with a roar,
Distributing a neat layer of clippings,
Well spread on the patio's floor.
The final phase comes with a blower,
The spread clippings attempting to clear,
From the patio's each nook and cranny,
A total failure for most times I fear.
All the while we remain at the table,
With our coffee and nice currant bun,
But never exchanging a single word,
Until the assault on our hearing is done.

When Feeling Sad

It's a comfort to sit, for an hour or so,
In the Mall centre court, where I often go;
When I'm lonely at home, in a mood rather blue,
Seriously thinking, about what I should do.
At the Mall I could sit, on a comfortable seat,
And at "2nd Cup Coffee", friends I may meet.
Then there are pleasures, if I happen to see,
A familiar mother and child, seated near me.
An adorable infant, with fine golden hair,
Who knows not my joy, at seeing her there.
So then I decide, as I'm feeling quite sad,
I should walk to the Mall, as the weather's not bad,
To see Rona and Sim, and just sit for a while,
Hoping to be cheered, by a golden child's smile.

ISBN 142510485-1

9 781425 104856